Valkyrie from tł

Basil Wells

Alpha Editions

This edition published in 2024

ISBN : 9789362094131

Design and Setting By
Alpha Editions
www.alphaedis.com
Email - info@alphaedis.com

VALKYRIE FROM THE VOID

By BASIL WELLS

**Staggering under the blasting heat of a great ringed
sun, she fought only to cross her savage slimy world.
The lithe Priestess Ylda knew not that her goal lay,
bright and shining, a thousand light-years away.**

Hardan Synn reined in his graceful golden-furred *maar* as he reached the rim
of the river's low bluff. He was uncomfortable, for the *vurth*-padded garments
that covered his naked body were growing dry, but tied to his huge hornless
saddle were three fat Dryland birds. He would eat well tonight.

The rough fare of cereals and preserved fish had palled. Five years of roaming
the blistering plains and mountains with sun-hardened prospectors and
hunters had given Hardan Synn a taste for Dryland flesh. So it was that he
quitted the camp when the day's trek was done and rode out in search of
game.

The maar's long black ears cupped forward, searching the source of some
discordant sound. Hardan's keen green eyes snapped back to the reality of
the camp sprawling half-in, half-out of the muddy bluish river.

Men were fighting, fists and clubs smashing into the down-furred flesh of
their fellows. The sound of their enraged bellowing and the shrill screams of
pain and agony grew louder even as he forced his maar down the steep path
to the bluff's base.

"Nitka Porn again," Hardan Synn spat out savagely as the blue dust swirled
about him. "Always he seeks to stir up trouble among the *sarifs*."

His sun-darkened face was a gaunt mask as he neared the river, but his slitted
green eyes were hot with growing rage. He could not leave the eighty great
wagons with their cargos of two hundred Wetlanders and their meager
supplies for so short a time as a *turev* of the water dial without trouble arising.

Hardan sprang off his mount and elbowed his way into the thick of the
melee, his broad hard shoulders tossing soggy-padded men aside. His hard
fists smashed one scowling-faced Wetlander's nose, and then he was through
into the rude square formed by the inner ring of six-wheeled wagons.

"Nitka Porn!" he shouted, his voice a knife-thrust of sound above the tumult.

The fighting men separated slowly, some weaving on their legs unsteadily,
bleeding, and others kneeling and groaning. A half-dozen, most of them

wearing the short green capes of the nobles' personal servants, sprawled limply in their own reddish-brown blood.

From one of these unmoving bodies a huge-bodied man, his brutal jaws masked by a bush of fiery red whiskers and his broad nose segmented by a sword-cut's diagonal scar, rose. Half his protective shell of faded blue cloth stuffed with vurth was ripped away from his shoulder and chest. Great muscles knotted there in his swiftly dehydrating pink flesh. He snarled at Hardan.

"The Drylander arrives," he jeered, and laughed.

From the hard-packed blue clay of the camping place he picked an arm-long stake of wood. He waved it derisively at Hardan.

"Watch him shiver," he roared. "When he is well beaten I will drive him from the camp. Then I will lead."

Hardan's stomach knotted—and then dissolved into a glowing spot of fire. His fingers bit into the leather handles of his twin short swords. He had no eyes for the grinning minority clustered about Nitka Porn. Nor did he see the puzzled empty faces of the other trekkers, the slow-minded plodding sarifs caught in this bloody trailside struggle.

"You stand alone against us all," snarled Nitka Porn, swaggering forward, his muddy green eyes slitted watchfully. "The Consars are dead, swimming in their fine wagon tanks for the last time. Their wagons and riding maars are ours now."

Hardan caught his breath on that. This was disaster!

"Fools," he said, his voice loud and sharp, "you know the price of any rebellion. The Consars will track you down. For many it will be the crushing death."

Even as he spoke his eyes never left those of the red-whiskered killer he fronted. In a moment the giant sarif would charge forward, his club swinging and the long curved sword of a dead lord in his other hand.

Hardan sprang to meet him, swords bared and gleaming. Perhaps with the death of Nitka Porn the revolt would collapse....

The stake caught him squarely on the shoulder. His left-hand sword dropped, tripping him. He caught himself, warded off a whistling slash of the huge curved blade of the sarif, and leaped backward. His left shoulder was numbed, his arm dangling limp as a blasted *netho* leaf in the noonday sun.

Hardan's sword darted in and out, flickering in the brazen sunlight. Blades clashed, slithered apart and the good steel rang clear as bells tinkling. Blood leaked through the pierced blue cloth of the sarif's vurth-padded garment in a half-dozen places.

His arm was tingling with reviving life. Through a red mist of hate Hardan fought with a cool machine-like series of lightning-swift lunges that ripped the sarif's skin into myriad reddish-brown furrows. Hatred was there, yes, but so controlled that it added strength to his sword arm and length to his blade.

The long curved sword flipped abruptly away into the faceless mass of the ringed trekkers. Nitka Porn pawed at his dripping knuckles, his mouth squared, his eyes bulging. He lunged backward, the men parting before his blind rush. And Hardan followed, his eyes hot.

"Kill him.... Mika, Garnd.... Don't let him.... No.... Mercy!" begged the great coward, his hands before his face.

Hardan poised his keen blade for the death thrust.

"No," he swore angrily, "by Ung Roth, I have not the heart for killing this foul *bladt*."

He rammed the sword into the clay. His fists swung hard, all the unleashed loathing and disgust of weeks past in their calculated blows, and Nitka Porn went down emptily, to quiver and lie still.

Hardan retrieved his swords, wiping the stains off on the unconscious hulk's ribboned cloth. He faced the sullen Wetlanders.

"I take over again," he announced. "Back to Aba we go. It's but two days' trek. There the guilty will be punished before I guide you to Lake Gron."

Dandu Mot, a gray-maned sarif, stepped forward. "No," he said simply. "We will not go back. The innocent would die with the guilty. And our children and women would be driven out of the settlement stripped of even our poor store of tools and food."

Hardan frowned. Dandu Mot was right. The justice of the Consars on the frontier was severe. They would make of this revolt a lesson for all that might follow along the arid dusty way from Wetland to Wetland. Even he, as guide and leader of the wagon train, might be killed.

The old man came closer, his faded green eyes pleading.

"We did not wish to revolt," he said. "It was Nitka Porn and his men who murdered the Consars. Perhaps beyond the Malsalm Range other Wetlands lie...."

His voice trailed off. Hardan's eyes swept over the oddly assorted throng of sarifs and craftsmen, poor oppressed men seeking a new and freer life beyond the Drylands. Could he see these sad-faced women made widows needlessly? And what of the young ones, their soft pelts as yet devoid of the scantiest of silky fur?

"I must yield," he said soberly. "And beyond the eastern uplands there does lie a sea. Only one Wetlander has ever looked upon it—Jaff Ka!" He paused. "By the grace of Ung Roth and Zo Aldan we may win through."

"There are Drylanders?"

Hardan nodded. "Drylanders who hide in watered valleys and war on all who venture there. Strange monsters, demons of Thog Molog, so say the Drylanders, lurk in the darkness to kill. And winged *soraps* that carry off half-grown children and woolly bladts."

"You know the way?"

"I have ridden across the Plateau of Fire to the Plains of Niid, Dandu Mot, but never to the Bitter Sea. But Jaff Ka told me the way."

"So let it be," said the old sarif, stroking his blistered cheek thoughtfully. "And, if we die in the Drylands—we at least die free!"

He turned to his followers. "Seize the followers of Nitka Porn and bind them. Tonight we will try them."

Swords and knives flashed. Clubs smashed and battered, and a moment later seven groaning men were led away. Four others of the red-bearded sarif's followers would walk no more, anywhere.

Hardan turned sharply on his heel and headed for the two wagons of the priests of Ung Roth Ka. His dehydrated body cried out for a soaking in the built-in tank in the wagon's middle. Only by frequent immersions and water-soaked outer shells of cloth could the Wetlanders endure the arid wastelands for more than a few hours.

A line of wounded, bruised men were already at the wagon, the two priests in their hooded orange cloaks attending to their hurts. And with the priests worked their gentle-faced wives, the priestesses of Zo Aldan Ra, the god's beloved mate. Hardan's blood pounded fast as he caught a glimpse of the white-robed novice, Ylda Rusla, bearing a steaming basin of water in her dainty hands.

"Hardan!" cried the girl, her soft green eyes lighting up, "you escaped death! You will take us back to Tarn—to safety?"

The frontiersman smiled down at the lithe full-breasted woman facing him. Even the soggy vurth-padded garments and the coarse white robe could not conceal the perfection of her body and face.

He shook his head.

"We go into the Malsalm Range," he told her, "and beyond."

"Not even to Lake Gron!" Ylda's face was ghastly. "But, I must—surely you could send me back."

"Sorry," Hardan muttered, "but you cannot leave us now. The wagon train must disappear—as though the Drylanders had attacked and destroyed it."

The girl's eyes flamed. "I command you to take me back to Aba!" Her foot stamped down imperiously.

"Ylda, believe me, I would if it were possible. But the lives of us all depend on absolute secrecy. No word of this train must ever reach the Consars of Tarn."

Ylda's small chin lifted and she turned her back, the hot water slopping down across her robe. She headed blindly back toward the wagons. Hardan shrugged, an empty pit in his middle. Any hope that he might win the beautiful novice from her devotion to Zo Aldan Ra was gone now.

He hurried past the wagons and down the blue clay slope to the fresh waters of the Gron River. For the moment he wanted no conversation with the priestly healers of the wagon train—or anyone else....

II

His body soaked luxuriously in the shady pool beyond a looming jut of reddish granite. Were his lungs drinking in the moist richness of the Upper Sea, the vurth-maintained mistiness above the true seas of Osar, he might have thought he was back in Tarn.

The Wetlands of Tarn were a handful of islands and a narrow thirty-mile-wide strip of foggy tropical plains and forests along the true sea of Tarn. Over the sea and back over the mainland extended the upper sea, a false sea of floating aerophyte growth, tenuous and frothy as spun threads of silvery moonbeams; yet capable of retaining a vast amount of moisture and warmth.

For almost a mile it extended upward, its delicate tendrils touching the restless sea and the fertile moistness of the land alike to draw life from them.

It offered no resistance to the passage of men or ships; yet it shielded them from the harshness of the vast ringed sun of Osar.

And here four million Wetlanders lived and built their dank massive-walled cities. Half of them were Tarns, ruled by the Council of Consars, and across the vastness of the Tarn Sea four other smaller kingdoms fought and squabbled over their narrow strips of vurth-shielded Wetland.

The land was overcrowded and so it came about that a few hardy adventurers pushed out into the Drylands. At first they followed the rivers, their bodies slowly toughening to the actinic rays of the direct sunlight, and later they struck out into the unknown dryness of grassy plains and deserts. They fought the huge apish Drylanders and ate the hairless horned ulfo of the plains and the woolly bladts of the barren hills.... And they found Lake Gron, where a large central island offered new homes for thousands of impoverished Consars and their sarifs.

So it was that endless series of wagon trains, drawn by domesticated Dryland beasts, maars and ulfos, pushed up the Aba River, and the Gron River beyond the dam at Aba, to the upland lake. And the hardy men of the frontier guided them—even as Earthmen ten centuries before, and a thousand light-years distant, had guided their effete Eastern countrymen into the Rockies and beyond....

Hardan stirred at last and climbed, refreshed, from his pool. Darkness had come and a dozen fires blazed merrily within the ringed double walls of the roofed wagons. He gathered up his weapons and clothing, wearing only the thin inner jerkin and trunks against the dryness of the night air, and went to the wagons.

Before dawn the wheels were rumbling and grinding up over the rock-strewn ridge above the river headed out into the eastern grasslands. The sleeping tanks, where the Wetlanders slept on moist elevated pads of vurth, were full and the spare water tanks were loaded as well. A dry trek of three, possibly four, days lay ahead of them before they could reach the eastward branching of the Aba River.

Hardan and three of the young sarifs stayed behind as the train moved away, readying the ten oldest wagons and the discarded equipment for the fire that was to help cover their tracks. Later parties of Wetlanders would find the ashes of wagons and the fire-blasted skeletons of men beside the trail and presume this had been a massacre by the apish barbarians of the plains.

"I wish the council of sarifs had ordered the death of Nitka Porn last night," said a blocky young sarif uneasily. "If they escape during the night there will be trouble."

Hardan touched his torch to the wagon they approached. The others were already ablaze. Together they swung into the saddles of their snorting maars. Only then did he speak.

"Yes, Malth Jed," he agreed. "It seemed to me that the council feared Nitka's wrath even though he was a prisoner. For that reason I advised Dandu Mot to double the guard."

"There was light from the fires last night," argued Malth Jed. "Why wait for daylight to slice their necks?"

"I do not believe all Porn's followers are prisoners," Hardan said grimly. "They may hope to free Nitka Porn and recapture the wagon train. Any delay would help that plot."

"Fools," grunted Malth Jed shortly. "The red-bearded one would turn on them even as he turned on the Consars."

By this time the other two sarifs had joined them on the rim of the bluff above the river. The wagons blazed up brightly, their sun-dried wood and cloth burning fiercely. With the morning sun only a smoking huddle of ashes and twisted metal would remain.

Hardan reined away from the bluff. They made too perfect targets against the illumination of the fire. But suddenly he arrested the little party's advance with a hiss of warning.

From the pale darkness before them the sound of distant shouts and shrieks came to them. The caravan was being attacked—or the outlaw sarifs had been freed!

"Spread out," Hardan commanded tensely, "as we reach the wagons. That way we will present a poorer target."

He dug his heels into the maar's sleek sides and they galloped forward along the rutted broad track of the wagon train.

The fighting had ended by the time they traversed the half mile gap that lay between them. The wagons were halted in a jumbled confused S-shaped tangle in the growing dawn. Only a sullen silence greeted them, but they saw dark movement against the slant-roofed bulk of the wagons.

"Hold!" warned Hardan. "Let me ride forward. It may be a trap."

And then, from a clump of wagons further along the snaking train, a maar and rider pounded out into the grasslands and headed in their direction. A man shouted something, and a confused chorus of yells answered him. After the lone rider a dozen other mounted men raced.

"It's a woman!" Malth Jed grunted, his bow ready in his thick fingers. "The white-robed novice of Zo Aldan Ra."

"Then they've overcome Dandu Mot and freed the red-bearded one," Hardan muttered, readying his own weapons.

The girl rode swiftly closer. The four riders went to meet her, their swords loosened in their sheaths and their spears in their hands. Only Malth Jed relied on his heavy hunting bow as a weapon; the others preferred throwing spears and swords.

"Hardan!" shrieked Ylda, "behind you!"

The frontiersman twisted in his saddle, a throwing spear grazed his vurth-padded shoulder, and he found himself facing the hate-twisted features of the two sarifs who had accompanied him. The strength of Nitka Porn in the wagon train must have been considerable, he thought ruefully, as he crossed swords with the lanky sarif on his left.

The sarif was no swordsman, the cowardly spear had been his only hope, and even as he turned his terrified eyes briefly toward his fellow an arrow bristled from the other sarif's throat. He shrieked and hurled his sword at Hardan even as he dug his heels into the maar's flanks. He went racing away, blood streaming from his sword-pierced upper arm.

Malth Jed reined closer. "Wound you?" Hardan shook his head.

"They killed Dandu Mot—many others—one of the holy healers who rebuked them—and now they loot the wagons." The girl's lips quivered as she spoke breathlessly.

"I guess you get your wish now, Ylda Rusla," he said grimly. "We ride back to Aba to ask for troops to pursue Nitka Porn."

Further conversation was impossible. The first pursuers, augmented now by a score or more of men on foot, were upon them. Spears and arrows were dropping around them as they wheeled their maars about to escape.

Ylda's maar went down, squealing horribly, a spear in her belly, and the girl was hurled over her mount's head into the tangled coarseness of the yellow ulfo grass. Before Hardan could swing back to scoop the unconscious body of Ylda from the ground their pursuers had reached her and surrounded her.

Hardan rode into them, hewing and slashing with his twin swords, letting his maar move as she willed. Blood splashed and spurted before his maddened blows, and the rebellious sarifs fell back momentarily. Ylda screamed. He saw a sarif on foot hoist the girl's struggling form to a mounted man, a huge-bodied redbeard, and the rider's fist smashing down at the juncture of rounded neck and fragile jaw.

Ylda went limp as Nitka Porn's blow landed and then the outlaw rode away, waving a derisive fist at Hardan across the bulwark of mounted men and attacking sarifs on foot.

He was battling for his life a second later. A spear found his body, and then another. Arrows hailed upward at him, piercing his padded limbs and drawing blood. In a moment he would be over-powered. Yet he fought on, trying to break through the press of rebel sarifs to pursue Ylda's captor.

"Hardan," a terrible voice roared above the shouts of his attackers, "escape.... Outnumbered!"

A spark of sanity remained in his weary brain. And the words of Malth Jed fanned it into life. His swords hissed, carving out a momentary gap, and he sent his maar plunging back the way they had come. He saw Malth Jed, sagging in his saddle, racing before him, and even as he watched a feathered shaft jutted abruptly from between his shoulderblades.

The stocky sarif slumped forward, clinging in his death agony to the saddle, and so they rode away into the growing daylight of the Drylands—a wounded cursing Wetlander and a jouncing bundle of dead sinews and bone that had once been a man....

Two hands of days had passed before Hardan dared leave the sheltered cave beside the Gron River not far from the ashes of the abandoned wagons. The two maars had pastured in a grassy hidden ravine and there too had he buried the stocky body of Malth Jed.

Then he had taken up the trail of the wagons again, and, despite the soreness of his half-healed wounds, come up with them in a matter of three days riding. He found them camped at the Isr River junction.

So now he lay on his belly in the early twilight, peering down into the rough circle of wagons, his eyes searching for the white-robed form of the girl he loved.

At last he saw her with one of the priests and a priestess sitting beside a small cooking fire apart from the others. But she no longer wore the garb of a novice. Instead she wore the green cloak of a Consar over her bulky vurth-stuffed coverings. A moment later he saw that her legs were linked by a short length of chain, riveted to either ankle by a cuff of metal. And across the fire squatted an armed man, a guard.

Hardan was puzzled at her change of garb, but his blood pounded with joy as he saw her apparently unharmed and well-fed. With the coming of darkness he could rescue her, and, Ung Roth willing, the priests and their wives as well.

So he set out looking for a concealed pathway to the river's edge and a thousand feet further downstream came upon a sheer gorge cut into the clay and soft gray rock of the bluff. Down this he lowered himself and in the increasing gloom made his way to the river and submerged.

He swam upstream, silent as a hunting *prel*, his only weapons his two swords. His spear and the excess garments he had left on the little sunken bowl of grass where his maars grazed.

Like a great Dryland Ape of the woodlands he crept up from the water at last, his only shelter the waist-high clumps of ulfo grass that dotted the river's shingly bank. And he won at last inside the carelessly guarded ring of wagons to the small fire where Ylda sat silently and stared into the flames.

From the shelter of a great double-spoked wheel he studied the camp. Well for the fleeing sarifs, he thought, that no raiding party of Drylanders had come to attack. He heard them quarreling and shouting drunkenly, and saw their swords and other weapons heaped carelessly beside the fires as they ate and caroused.

The guard spat impatiently into the fire and ran a dry tongue over his parched lips. Longingly he studied the growing excitement at the center of the encampment. There was nothing to do here, only the priest and priestess discussing the strange healing property of a vegetable mold recently discovered in Tarn. He slapped his hip, cursed roughly, and climbed to his feet.

"Don't stir from the fire," he ordered Ylda fiercely. His tongue poked thirstily at his lips.

The guard swaggered away from the fire toward the curtain-hung rear of the wagon just ahead. This wheeled canvas-and-wood shack had a sagging roof sloping from a central ridge to either end of the box so that a sort of awning covered the low rear entrance. He reached inside and when his arm emerged a basket-woven jar was in his hand, its inner earthware lining containing a sloshing fluid.

Hardan scented the raw reek of alcohol, of *garack*, as he crept closer. The guard's thick lips smacked, he rubbed a rasping fist across his mouth and snorted appreciatively. Then the jar tilted again, gurgled.

The guide sprang, his fingers clamping about the startled throat of the sarif. He squeezed hard, choking back the gasp of terror, and the jug crashed to the hard ground. Then his fist chopped in a short vicious punch to the sarif's neck that felled the man.

He trussed the sarif swiftly with his own filthy brown cape, stuffing a generous handful into the gaping mouth, before he crossed to the fire and squatted in the guard's place.

Ylda came to her feet, hand to her mouth.

"Hardan!" She came toward him jerkily, the chain making her take mincing, careful steps.

"Sit down," he told her. "And warn your friends to keep their places." The priest and the priestess smiled quietly.

"Fear nothing from us," they told him. "Our calling is to heal the bodies and minds of the sick. It was for that mighty Ung Roth Ka came from the greater of the four moons to dwell among men. We care nothing for the quarrels and jealousies of men."

"Though," added the priestess, "as a woman and not a servant of Zo Aldan Ra, I hope you escape safely."

The priest nodded, his eyes twinkling. "We are yet only human. Though we will not use violence yet we can give advice and appeal to our mighty master in your behalf."

Hardan bowed, his hand making the respectful sign of a believer on the great god of healing. "I will bind you before we leave," he said, "unless you will come with us."

The priest shook his head. "There are many sick and fearful in the train," he said, "we remain to aid them."

Hardan turned to Ylda. "After I break your chain slip beneath the wagon and through the grass to the river. I will follow."

He arose and came over to her as though to examine her bonds. His hands clamped the chain and he tested the hand-forged links. One of them twisted and spread apart. Quickly he wrapped a strip of her green cape around either length of chain and her leg.

Ylda slipped away. Hardan busied himself binding the priest and priestess of the only gods and then followed. Almost he had reached the river when the silvery light of the four moons of Osar shone from beneath a pear-shaped cloud above the distant eastern hills.

Instantly the river flats were lighted bright as their beloved Wetlands. And a guard, rousing from his half-sleep in the white brilliance, saw Hardan's moving shape. He cried a warning.

Hardan knew the need for stealth was gone now. He ran to the river bank where Ylda waited, took her hand, and flung himself out into the sluggish muddy stream. He swam directly across and there, taking her in his arms, headed into the vine-tangled growth of scrub *ossa* and knotty *brel*. And at its edge he halted long enough to send a shout of defiance back at the clustering sarifs.

After that he wasted no more breath. Downstream he threaded his way until a crook in the river piled a welcome wall of blue clay and shale between the camp and them. Here he again took to the river and a few minutes later they were running breathlessly across the moonlit plain beyond toward the hidden maars.

"Tricked them that time," chuckled Hardan, saddling their mounts. "We'll circle eastward toward the Blue Malsalms and then head back toward Aba."

Ylda put her slim fingers on Hardan's arm and squeezed. It told him, more than words, that she was happy to have escaped and that as yet she was breathless.

He lifted her into the saddle and then mounted himself. It was so easy now— a day's ride away from the river and then a southward swing until they could head directly westward back toward Aba and the river trail to the Wetlands....

The rocky escarpment loomed closer and closer as they drove their lathered maars up the boulder-strewn slope. Ylda turned for a hasty glance backward.

"They're gaining, Hardan," she shouted.

"It'll be night soon," Hardan called back, "and the Drylanders fear darkness." But his eyes probed vainly for a way of escape ahead.

His mouth twisted wryly as he recalled his plan of the preceding night. At midday a mounted party of the giant Drylanders, savage yellow-haired, apish brutes, had sighted them and for the last five hours they had found safety only in swift flight. Now, unless a gorge or pass opened in the looming grayness of the brown-splotched cliffs, they were trapped at its base.

Already the triumphant scrawling of the Drylanders sounded in their ears as the ape-things fanned out on either hand. Once that curved line pinned them against the cliff they were trapped, to be killed or, if captured alive, saved for sacrifice to the foul god of the Drylands, Thog Molog.

The sheer escarpment loomed higher and more forbidding as they neared it. Hardan felt his chest grow hollow as the last prospect of escape dwindled. All that remained now was to find a vantage point above their pursuers and sell their lives dearly. To be taken alive was unthinkable.

A huge flat-topped boulder shouldered the cliff, its rim twenty feet above the sandy soil, and toward this Hardan led the way. It was a natural fort that they might hold until darkness clamped down.

Hardan rode his maar close up to the rock, where a crevice split several feet diagonally down the face of the boulder, and swung up from the saddle. A moment later he was crouched on the rock helping Ylda to his side.

Their maars moved away only a few paces and started grazing on the sparse-leaved clumps of ossa and brel at the cliff's base. Hardan turned, facing the cliff, and now he saw an opening in the cliff wall where the boulder's flat rim touched it. It was a low oval of darkness going back deep into the cliff's heart, a cave entrance hid by the great rock.

"In, quickly," he ordered Ylda, "before the Drylanders arrive."

And hardly had they reached that welcome shelter than the huge warriors came thundering up to the cliff.

At sight of the empty saddles the Drylanders growled their amazement, their guttural meager speech carrying excited overtones of superstitious terror. Hardan understood enough of their brutish gabble to learn that they believed their monster god, Thog Molog, had carried them away.

Then keen tiny eyes discovered the flat-roofed boulder and a moment later their shadowy hiding place was discovered. Instantly the hushed mutterings and moans of awe changed to roars of rage. They came swarming up over the rock.

Hardan met them with arrows and spears. The first wave of attackers fell back, only to launch a second and more powerful assault. This time they swung up to the boulder-top together and the Wetlander dropped back into the cave-mouth, his twin swords bared.

The apish giants crouched down and came raging at him, only to be spitted on his flashing blades until the opening was choked with bloody chilling flesh. Their comrades dragged the bodies backward and once the orifice was cleared flung themselves at him again.

His swords bit deep, drinking the life of Drylander after Drylander until at last the assault ceased. Darkness had fallen and the great brutes had lost their stomach for further battle. So they withdrew, taking their dead with them, and built three fires of dry brush and cactus about the uprear of the huge rock.

His swords bit deep, drinking their lives.

"And that's that tonight," panted Hardan, wiping his swords mechanically of the blood that smirched their keen blades.

In the darkness Ylda's soft hands ran over his arms and chest searching for wounds. His blood ran hot as her soft flesh met his.

"You're untouched!" she cried, unbelieving.

"Had all the advantage," Hardan scoffed. "But if we're here when the sun rises again—we won't be so lucky."

Ylda peered out, her eyes reading the purpose of the three fires. Placed so they effectively ruled out any escape in the darkness, the Drylanders on guard would see instantly any movement atop the rock. Her breath caught in her throat and she clung to Hardan's sweat-damp body.

"We'll try the cave," Hardan told her thickly, very conscious of her intimate nearness. "It may have another entrance higher or beyond the cliff."

Roughly he broke away from the girl and started back into the darkness, his swords probing the gloom. And behind him he heard the girl following. The floor was uneven, rough patches of rock, and so, she stumbled before she had come a dozen paces.

After that her hand clung to his crossed sword-belts as the way climbed gradually higher.

Echoes of their passage grew more distant. The cavern roof and walls must be drawing away on all sides. Hardan licked his dry lips and the parched dryness of his vurth-padded body sapped his strength. They halted for a moment to finish the last of their water bags and munch a tough strip of dried ulfo meat before pushing on.

"We must find water soon," whispered Ylda faintly, "or I am finished."

And a short distance further along Hardan felt her fingers slip from their grip on his belt. She lay silent and limp on the rocky floor, her soft skin harsh and dry as the Dryland hills, and her cracked lips moaning.

He lifted her and staggered onward. His years in the Drylands had toughened his flesh and lungs to withstand the arid violence of the grasslands for several hours, but even yet he must sleep in or near water at night. He suffered mightily, his lungs on fire and his throat a dust-rasping channel. Like a man in a grotesque nightmare of torture he felt his wooden limbs move uncertainly far below him.

Only when the stars were above him and he felt the welcome fluidity of water about his parched ankles did he halt and lower the girl. The water was chill but his thirsty body sucked at it greedily.

III

The huge ringed sun of Osar was yet hugging the rim of the ragged Malsalm's peaks to the east when he awoke, shivering despite the thick dampness of his vurth-stuffed covering. Behind him, wedged against the rocky shelf and protected by a down-curving slab of rock, huddled Ylda.

He slipped off his thick shell and heaped it on the girl's sleeping body for additional warmth and stepped out, naked as go the men of the Upper Seas in their moist-walled cities and lush meadows. As yet the sun was not too warm for his sleek-furred flesh.

They had come up from the cliff to a narrow long plateau atop it. A shallow rocky lake was at their feet and a stream came down from a snow-capped peak in the southern distance to feed its chill moistness. Abruptly he remembered the cave and the yellow-haired Dryland giants who trailed them.

A long crevice rifted the floor of the miniature tableland not far from the lake's brim. Perhaps in the rainy season the overflow of the lake found escape there, but now it was dry, a crude staircase dipping down into the gloomy abyss that was the cave they had traversed. Hardan sensed the immensity of the void beneath, the whole cliff must be a honeycomb of caverns and subterranean passages.

The sound of horny bare feet and the rubbing of metal on the leather of harness warned him that the Drylanders had overcome their aversion of the darkness enough to trail them. He caught a glimpse of a moving blob of blackness that could only be them a hundred feet and more below.

Hardan laughed. The rift was walled with heaps of rocky debris, boulders brought down from the poles in glacial eras and sections of splintered igneous rock. He put his arm and shoulder against them and heaved. He sang lustily as he worked.

One after another they fell, the smaller ones entering the crevice and bounding downward to rip the climbing Drylanders from their hold; the others clogging forever the way from below. He rolled a last rounded boulder of green-shot basaltic origin and turned, hand at his sword.

Ylda was standing there, his vurth-padded garment's ugliness in her extended hands. She smiled, her eyes warm in the shadow of her wide-rimmed quilted headgear of vurth. Suddenly Hardan was aware of the growing intensity of the morning sunlight parching his down-covered flesh. In his excitement he had forgotten the blistering sun.

He slipped quickly into the coverall-like covering, its dampness doubly welcome after his exposure to the deadly atmosphere of the Drylands, and went with her to the rim of the narrow flat-roofed ridge where they had climbed.

"We can't go back, Ylda," he told her, his hand pointing out the way they had come up across the arid lands from the Isr River.

Ylda's eyes swung northward and then on around to the south again. She shuddered and Hardan sensed her terror of this molten naked hell of tortured rock and waterless slope that hemmed them in.

"We'll follow this stream up to its source," he went on after a moment, "and then find another that flows westward toward the Gron or the Aba. Nothing to it."

The girl's lips twisted in a tremulous attempt at a smile.

"Hardan," she said, "before you start back with me I must tell you why I was held captive by the rebelling sarifs."

Hardan shook his head, his mind raging. There could be only one reason for her to be in chains. Nitka Porn had wanted her and until she would consent to be his woman she might escape. That could be the only truth, he thought, and he wanted to hear nothing about it.

"But I must tell you, Hardan, before you—before we—leave the mountains. I was going to Lake Gron to meet my lover. He is a Consar, Serid Jern."

"Serid Jern!" snapped out Hardan. "That beak-nosed gray-haired old wastrel! You mean you—he was your lover?"

"But let me explain. It's not what you think. There is nothing wrong. He is a Consar and my father...."

"Enough." Hardan jerked her along by the arm. "I wish to hear no more about it. You are young and knew no better. When we reach Aba I will carry you away in the lawful manner."

Ylda's slight body stiffened and she pulled away from Hardan angrily. "Don't touch me again, ever!" she cried.

Hardan shrugged and headed off up the lake toward the stream that fed it. If the obstinate little sarif girl wanted to follow him let her. He had almost forgotten that he was born into an impoverished Consar family, these last few years, but now he remembered the vast social gulf between them. Yet he would gladly have given up his rank had Ylda agreed to mate with him.

And now she scorned him. It was as though she were the Consar and he the sarif. The months she must have spent with the priests and priestesses of Ung Roth and Zo Aldan had given her a false conception of a woman's place on Osar.

Let her have her soft-bellied old lover in Gron Lake. She'd get her fill of battling the half-dozen other sarif girls he'd collected there already....

Hardan's knuckles whitened on the handles of his swords, and he cursed all the Serid Jerns of the Wetlands.

Abruptly he came to a halt. Beside the rough trail he followed a peculiar-looking dwarfish creature lay sleeping at the stream's brink. His body was hairless, save on the top of his skull and under his nose and on his cheeks, and he was weaponless save for a short thick bow and a club. A cloak of muddy green covered his tattered unpadded coveralls.

Hardan stirred the sleeping creature with his toe and it sat up. He spoke to it in Tarnish, and in the scanty tongue of the great Dryland Apes. And at this the sunken monkeylike little eyes blinked with a certain measure of intelligence. It rose to its meager six feet of height and faced him.

"I am called Kern Rensom," he cried shrilly. "I am from Aarth," his puny arm made an indefinite circling motion. "Long ago we came to Osar to conquer it all."

Hardan grinned. "Little Drylanders like you better keep hid or the winged soraps will carry you off. You couldn't lick a couple of bladts."

The little Aarthman's arms and body flashed into movement so swift that Hardan could not see what was happening. He felt himself flying through the air and jolted down a dozen paces away, his breath gone. He heard Ylda's amused laughter, and the sound spurred him to bound to his feet and leap toward the little man.

Ylda cried out in protest—the Aarthman had drawn no weapon but stood with arms folded—and Hardan's pace slowed. He could not run through a man who would not protect himself.

"Take up your club!" he cried savagely, "or one of my swords!"

The little man grinned impishly, his wide mouth red in the uncouth tangle of his scrubby brown whiskers.

"Try to hit me," he invited.

Hardan's anger overcame his scruples. He swung his right hand sword in an arc that would have bit a respectable nick out of the Aarthman's shoulder. And the sword seemed to freeze in midair!

He fought against the paralysis that froze his muscles. Sweat salted his face and body as he threw all his strength into the effort, but he could not stir. Nor could he move his legs or the other arm. After a long moment of struggle he recognized his efforts were useless and ceased his frantic mental commands. And in that instant his body was free again.

"Are you a man or one of the devil-things of Thog Molog?" he demanded fearfully, sheathing his blade.

"I am like yourself, Hardan Synn," said the little man, amused. "But I have mental power that you of Osar cannot comprehend. It is the only weapon of Aarth we are permitted to use."

"You—you called me by name!" Hardan cried out. "Now I know you are of Thog Molog's foul brood. Only a devil-thing could be at once so puny and so hideous."

"You are wrong, Hardan," and now Kern Rensom used words that were a blend of Dryland and Wetland speech. "I can look into your mind and understand what you think. Even now I can tell you that you misjudge Ylda Rusla."

"No!" broke in the girl, "please keep silent, strange man."

Kern Rensom shrugged. "As you wish," he said. He turned to Hardan again.

"Perhaps you can come with me to my home valley before returning to Aba." He laughed at the unspoken refusal in Hardan's brain. "We have a small lake in the crater covered with an upper sea of vurth," he added.

"Why not?" demanded Ylda. "For too long have I breathed the harsh upland air. To move unencumbered through the soft dampness of the vurth sea would be heaven."

Hardan nodded doubtfully. "Very well," he said. "But remember it means the revolting sarifs may escape beyond the Blue Balsalms."

"I hope they do," flashed Ylda, "and you do too. Most of the sarifs are good people. Even if Nitka Porn and a few others escape punishment the innocent ones will escape."

"That's settled then." Hardan turned to the Aarthman. "Lead off, Kern Rensom."

And so they started off eastward across the mountains and bare reddish-veined slopes of the blue ridges, the tiny Aarthman leading. All forenoon they walked, pausing often beside the stream to soak their padded garments and gather the sparse scattering of brown-husked berries from bushes in the sheltered angles of the little watercourse.

Toward noon they left the swift little stream and crossed a steep slope of treacherous yellow shale and broken rock to a slope that carried them down toward a vast sunken bowl, an extinct crater, in whose heart the misty outlines of a small lake nestled grayly. That it was roofed with vurth there could be no question, and thereafter Hardan forgot most of his suspicions that the stranger meant them evil.

"It was there," Kern Rensom said, his finger pointing out a squatty ovoid of darker rock, "that our ship from beyond the stars landed. It was broken, and all save two women and one man died."

"You came from up there?" demanded Ylda. "Then you are of the race of the true gods, Zo Aldan and Ung Roth?"

The Aarthman shook his head. "No, we are mortals. I have read your mind and learned about your gods. Perhaps your gods, too, were mortals from another world who landed here safely on Osar."

Hardan's ears tingled at such heresy. And yet he was forced to admit what the little man said was logical. He knew that many of the wisest Wetlanders did not believe in Thog Molog and the devil-things, nor did he suppose the Drylanders believed in the power of Zo Aldan and Ung Roth. It was true the two gods had come from the outer moons in a strange metallic ship.

"Why then," he asked, "did you not conquer the Drylands? Was it not for that you came to Osar?"

Kern Rensom tugged at his scrubby beard. "We were too few at first. And when there were a thousand of us we tried to use the weapons and tools we had sealed away, but we had forgotten. All the juice that powered them had seeped away. Nor could we repair them."

"But you have books," insisted Hardan. "They would tell you."

The little man was shamefaced. "While we waited; hunting, building our city, and tilling our fields, we forgot how to read. For many centuries we have lived on a level but little above that of the Drylanders."

Hardan swore with amazement. Despite their wonderful mental power these Aarthmen were little better than ignorant savages. Perhaps if he could bring a few wise men from the Wetlands to this valley and have them work with the Aarthmen they could reconstruct that forgotten language and learn to build ships that flew in the air.

With great ships like theirs the journey from Wetland to Wetland would be simple and all Osar would be opened to them. No longer would they be forced to haul sleeping tanks of water by slow wagons across the dry-grassed plains....

The trail wound aimlessly, it seemed to Hardan, down into the vast circular abyss of the crater. And after a time, as they neared the lower slopes, he saw the Aarthman scratch his shaggy brown head in apelike fashion, and stop.

"You've lost your way," he told Kern.

Kern Rensom nodded. "I escaped from a small band of Roons, the Drylanders who dwell on the slopes above our craters, two days ago. I was hunting on the northern side and was forced to circle southward to where you found me."

"But if we continue downward we must come to your city," Hardan said, puzzled. "Why do you hesitate?"

"All Smeth Valley is surrounded by a high wall, Hardan, built by my people. But on the southern inner slope for more than a mile an ancient, higher wall was there. A wall circling down to the lake.

"Since we came to Smeth Valley only a few men have ventured beyond that wall, and of them all only one returned—a madman!"

"You think we are approaching that section then?" Hardan laughed and his hands found comforting grip on his sword hilts. "Nothing could lie beyond there save deserted ruins," he scoffed.

"Perhaps we could walk along the wall's rim," Kern said, disregarding Hardan's laughter, "until we passed the walled-in section. The ridges on either side crowd up to the wall so it would be our only path."

"That'd be better than climbing up again," agreed Hardan.

And so, a dozen tortuous bends in the deepening ravine they followed, later, they fronted the soaring smooth-jointed face of a gigantic wall. At their feet the dry bed of the ravine ended in solid granite, and on either hand the ravine's walls lifted sheer for fifty feet and more.

Try as they would they could not climb the craggy walls. Apparently they were to be forced to return back along the way they had come and find some new path to the lower crater depths.

Ylda cried out and pointed to the lower part of the pierced vertical slab set in the wall before them. The scanty flow of freshets here in the uplands had slowly worn away a larger hole, a process that must have consumed unthinkable centuries, until even a Wetland warrior could have wriggled through.

Hardan nodded. He too had seen the opening but did not want to suggest using it. The Aarthman's fantastic tale had affected him more than he cared to admit. Now he knelt down and thrust his head carefully through the orifice.

"Just a grassy slope," he called back, his voice loud with relief. "Down by the lake there's a jumble of rock slabs and columns, could be a city. Not even any trees until the upper sea begins."

He withdrew his head and slid through feet-first, dropping into a deep wide rocky pocket gouged out by the ravening mountain torrents. Ylda followed, slipping into his arms easily, but her face turned away stiffly as he set her on her feet. Hardan growled and turned away, disgusted at the little sarif's continued show of dislike.

"Hurry up, Kern Rensom," he said.

The Aarthman's be-whiskered face appeared. Under that brushy brown stubble his brown skin had paled to a strangely green shade.

"I don't know," he said uncertainly. "The Drylanders claim this is the abode of Thog Molog. I've seen crude pictures of their god. It's a many-armed ghastly monster bigger than a Drylander's communal *yad*."

Hardan too sensed the alien silence and remoteness of this close-cropped expanse of sward. Almost he expected to see a flock of the woolly, vari-colored bladts grazing there, so close was the brook-watered grass trimmed to its roots. Something, ancient foul things, must lurk in those brooding ruins and come out in the moonlight to eat. No grass could grow so uniform and short.

So they moved together, speaking no more, through the hushed silence of growing dusk, into the shadows of the vast vertical mass of the ancient wall that dipped southward. They searched for a way to scale that soaring obstacle, vainly.

The rim of the upper sea, the false sea that was vurth floating lightly above the true sea far below, they reached and Hardan felt the tingling thrill of a stranger returning home as the delicate moist tendrils contacted his exposed flesh. He heard Ylda's sigh of sensuous ecstasy as she sucked in the dank richness of the confined atmosphere, and he heard the Aarthman breathing unsteadily as though half-choked.

"How you can stand this pea-soup," came the little man's strangled voice, "is beyond me. It's like walking underwater; yet breathing."

Hardan laughed and slipped out of his cumbersome padded garb. Now he could climb the wall or fight more freely. The intangible unseen menace of the walled city and fields now struck him with returned power. He bound the suit into a pack on his shoulders and set about examining the damp and crumbling wall. The moisture had loosened its ancient bonding material and he found many foot and hand holds.

Swiftly he angled upward, his two companions following the way he had found. Once he ran into a section of intact wall and was forced to turn back, and Ylda swung upward along a new series of crevices, leading the way. Hardan now brought up the rear instead of Kern Rensom.

The vurth ended, and even as they saw that less than twenty feet lay between them and the wall's top, a hideous gagging squelching sound, like a mud-wallowing drunkard venting his addled rage, sounded from below.

Hardan turned to look down, his sword in his right hand and his feet jammed in a shallow crack.

A vast bulk, indistinct in the failing light of the vanished sun, and rendered yet more vague by the aerophytic sea that washed around its lower body, reared there. Hardan sensed that the greasily smooth hide, wet and slime-covered, was slate-gray, liberally splotched with patches of ghastly pale yellow. He saw an inner gaping maw, its huge inner jaws covered with bony serrated ridges, and in a deadly fringe about this mouth a score or more of specialized tentacles stretched like multi-jointed arms upward.

"Climb swiftly!" roared Hardan, "while I hold it back."

The tentacles slithered nearer, their gray snaky flesh ending at the tips in sucker-like yellow-tinged discs. Hardan swung his weapon down at the nearest and from the severed tentacle tip a steaming purplish ichor spurted. And with its wound the burbling mouthings from below redoubled.

The Wetlander sprang upward, a questing tentacle brushing his heel as he found a new vantage point several feet higher, and then he sliced through this leathery appendage's tip as well.

But now three of the tentacles wormed together at him, and though his blade slashed off two of them, the third found his naked flesh and the suction discs ripped at him. He clung to the wall, his discarded sword clattering downward, but relentlessly the monster was dragging him from his precarious perch.

He heard a sob at his side and his other sword was drawn from its sheath even as his left hand lost its grip. Then he was released, the tentacle tip yet clinging to his flesh, and he found Ylda tugging at his arm. The Aarthman lowered his bow and Hardan pushed the trembling girl up to him.

A moment later they were all three safe a scant four feet above those questing hungry ropes of flesh, and Ylda was in his arms....

IV

Moonlight silvered white the inner crater when they reached the Aarth city. The gates were closed and Kern Rensom said they would not be opened until the dawn. He guided them to a hunting estate owned by his older brother, a well-to-do Aarthman farmer, that was not far from the upper sea's rim and there they left him.

That night they slept in a soft mound of hastily gathered Wetland moss, the thick wetness of the upper sea closing about them like a warm blanket. And for long Hardan lay awake, his blood singing with the knowledge that Ylda's love was his.

Their escape from the penned-in monster, the Drylanders' fabled Thog Molog, had broken through the barriers of her false pride and she had confessed that she loved him. And she had explained to him that she was really the daughter of a noble landowner who had been courted by the aging Serid Jern against her parents' wishes. She had disguised herself as a sarif girl and joined the priestesses as a novice to reach Lake Gron and her husband-to-be.

"But I am glad I met you, Hardan," she had whispered, "before I mated with him. I could not have really loved him; only the glamour of his wild frontier kingdom attracted me.

"Nor will my father object to my marrying a sarif. He holds that the man himself is of more importance than his rank."

Hardan smiled, before he went to sleep, at the reversal in his position. Now he was the sarif, rather than Ylda. Nor did he intend to tell her of his equal rank until they stood together before her father....

With morning they left the upper sea and with the Aarthman made their way to the city. Here the diminutive men and women made much of them, feting and dining them, and learning all they could of the Wetland civilization they had never before contacted.

Kern Rensom showed them the buildings where the corroded tools of their ancestors were stored so carefully, and he took them inside the twisted wreckage of the space ship on the slope above the city. Most of all was Hardan interested in the metallic-leaved books and stacks of circular containers of record tape. Here was the secret of the Aarthmen if they but had the key of written words to unlock it.

The pictures interested him as well. The Aarthmen owned several worlds: cloud-swathed, green-clad continents and vurthless broad seas, and a dying red world of deserts. And their sun was a tiny red ball without the least sign of an outer solar ring. How much more beautiful was Osar's generous ringed luminary, thought the Wetlander.

So it was that they spent day after day in the peaceful valley of the Aarthmen, cementing the bonds of friendship that Hardan hoped would release the forgotten knowledge of Aarth for both races. Almost had he forgotten the toiling caravan of huge six-wheeled wagons that even now must be traveling through the waterless desolation of the passes of the Blue Malsalm Range to the north.

"You should be told, Hardan," Kern Rensom said, as the mounted messenger rode off down the broad paved street, "that the wagon train you guided has halted less than a day's journey to the north. And the evil-brained sarif, Nitka Porn, has laid a trap for the small party of soldiers who pursue them."

Hardan's eyes flashed. It was not enough that Nitka Porn had taken over control of the train. Now he must slaughter more Wetlanders instead of attempting escape. He realized that he must kill the huge-bodied sarif before he could cause any more bloodshed and misery. Perhaps there was yet time to rescue the doomed warriors.

"One of our hunters crept close enough to the wagon train to catch the thoughts of Nitka Porn," the little man was saying. "The attack is to be late today or in the morning."

"Kern Rensom!" cried Hardan, "could you get me a guide and maars to take me to the soldiers?"

"I can do better," grinned the Aarthman. "I can come along. And bring a score of warriors as well."

Hardan took his sword-belts down from their pegs and buckled them on. He looked to his bow and replaced the somewhat frayed string. Then he strode out the door to where the maars they had ridden earlier in the morning were kept. And with him walked the little Aarthman, clean-shaven now and dandified in embroidered blouse and wide-bottomed trousers of woven blue fabric. He too was hooking on his harness of knives, arrow quiver, and throwing club.

They mounted, pulling their desert robes from behind the saddles—this last was an Aarth invention that shielded them from sunglare and stinging sand flurries—and rode toward the poorer section of Smeth City where hunters and warriors lived. Nor were they long in recruiting a force of thirty mounted men and leaving the city behind.

Yet as they reached the great gate in the towering outer wall, the wall that barred the lower crater to any but Aarthmen, a wide-hatted rider with desert robes high about his face, awaited them. And as they filed through the narrow slot the sliding gate-slab permitted this rider to join the party.

Hardan rode close to the stranger and uncovered the shielded features. He shrugged and shouted across to Kern Rensom.

"I might have known," he laughed. "It is Ylda."

"Why should I not go?" she demanded. "Perhaps it is my father or my brother who commands the soldiers. They were to be assigned to the Aba River command this term."

"So!" Hardan nodded. "You tire of us and wish to go with them. Or perhaps you wish to find them so we can mate."

The high color that flooded Ylda's downy haired cheeks was answer enough. Her chin elevated proudly, but she said nothing. And Hardan too hoped her father was serving his year, every sixth year a Consar was supposed to enter the armed forces of Tarn, for that much the sooner could they be mated.

Through the gate they rode and up increasingly dry barren slopes until they reached the jumbled hell of ridges, splintered crevices, and ragged gorges that lay above the crater's rim. They rode through the midday heat, pausing but once to soak their dehydrated garments of padded vurth in a cave-hidden pool, and then onward again until the shadows on their right grew long and dark.

"It is near," the Aarthman who guided them said. He dismounted. "Here we must leave our maars and proceed on foot if we are to surprise the sarifs."

The little party obeyed, glad of the opportunity to stretch cramped stiff limbs. They followed along a narrow shallow gorge to where it opened into a larger sunken pass. Down there, in a rock-strewn boxlike cavity, they saw movement.

"We are too late," Hardan muttered to Ylda. "Shiny leather shells and metal caps are those of Wetland soldiers. It is they who are trapped in that hollow."

Now they could see the sarifs just below their own vantage point. They clustered at either end of the cliff-walled trap, their arrows and the jagged boulders they had collected effectively barring any attempt by the soldiers to cut their way through. Already more than half the Tarnish fighting men were down, and it was but a matter of time until the last of them died.

Further to the east, in a stream-watered little park, the wagons were bulked in a rude circle. They were fewer now, less than thirty were left of the original train, and they were patched and travel-stained. "We had better divide, Kern Rensom," said Hardan thoughtfully. "You take ten men and take cover above the western party. I will take the others to capture the wagons and the other party."

"Good," agreed the little man from Aarth, and he started issuing orders at once.

Taking advantage of whatever cover the broken nature of the uplands afforded, the Aarthmen and the Wetlanders slipped downward toward the sarifs. Nor were they detected before they had reached a bulging ridge of flinty red rock twenty feet above them.

Hardan cupped his hands and shouted down at the fifteen ragged men below, "Throw down your weapons, sarifs. You are surrounded."

The men turned, startled, to look upward into the eyes of twenty strange little men and the two Wetlanders. Nor could they fail to see the arrows that centered on their vitals. One by one they loosed their bows and spears, their nerveless fingers twitching.

Nowhere could Hardan see Nitka Porn, though he counted five of the rebel sarifs immediate underlings in the group.

"Where is Nitka Porn?" he demanded.

The sarifs stirred uneasily, their sullen green eyes shifting and their tongues dabbing at blackened cracked lips. They were a hopeless, stupid-looking crowd. From them the Drylands had sapped their strength and sucked dry their brains. Nor had the browbeating of Nitka Porn been without influence in this final result.

One of them, a broken-toothed oldster who feared the rebel sarif the less because he was so near to death, stepped clumsily forward.

"He is at the wagons, Hardan." The reedy old voice trembled. "So securely were the soldiers trapped that he knew they must die. He went for wagons to carry the loot."

"Good, Vesko Rok," said Hardan. "Now I would ask you more. Come aside with me."

The old sarif shuffled after Hardan out of earshot of the others. Quickly he demanded the names of all the sarifs loyal to Nitka Porn in this and the other group. Then he gave orders to separate the prisoners.

"Nolson," he said to one of the sturdy little men of Aarth, "I want you to remain here with ten men. Guard well these seven sarifs."

The Aarthman's blue eyes were bright. "They will not escape," he said.

"The others we are taking back to the wagon train," Hardan told him, and set out along the rugged path down toward the camp.

Nitka Porn came riding out of the camp with two others of his men. They were all three fat and healthy-looking. They had fared better than the rest of the party, riding much of the day in the tank baths of the wagons and eating the best of the food.

Behind them rolled three wagons, the teams of bony maars pulling them driven by women. Apparently all the able-bodied sarif males had been forced to join the ambushers.

When they came opposite the Aarthmen and the sarif prisoners stepped out from their concealing boulders and rocks, the show of weapons by the little hairless men of Aarth sufficient to make the whole force seem armed.

"I want you, Nitka Porn." Hardan's voice was slow, his pent-up rage well under control.

The huge sarif's freckled face was mottled with fear and hatred. His yellowish-green eyes were baleful as he swung down from the saddle. Hardan's ears heard a rush of feet and then a ghastly series of shrieks and thuddings, and from the corner of his eye saw the other two horses were now riderless. The sarifs were trampling at something underfoot and the Aarthmen were turning away pale sickened faces from what was there.

Ylda's hand was on his arm. "Take him prisoner," she begged. "Tarnish justice will punish him. And he is so big, so brutal—you will be killed!"

Hardan pushed gently at her arm. Nitka Porn was a spear's length away now and his swords were drawn. Then, before Hardan could stop her, Ylda had stepped between them.

"Surrender your weapons, Nitka Porn," she commanded imperiously, "and you will live to see Aba."

Nitka's flat-nosed simian face snarled. "Surrender and be torn apart as were they?" His head nodded toward the mumbling knot of crazed sarifs beside the terrified maars. He laughed hoarsely, and with one great arm swept the girl close.

One of his swords now pressed against the breast of Ylda, ready to plunge deep into her vitals. He backed again toward his maar.

"At the first sign of attack," he told Hardan, "the woman dies."

He prepared to climb into the saddle, to ride away into the eastern uplands that led toward the Desert of Niid and the Bitter Sea that had been their goal. And then it was that Hardan remembered the strange power of the Aarthmen.

No sooner had the thought been born in his brain than the little men chuckled and their dejected faces brightened. Nitka Porn's body froze immobile and slowly he spread his arms so the girl stepped free.

"Enough," Hardan called. "Release him and let him fight for his life."

"Better that we should make him slice his own throat," muttered one of the Aarthmen, but unwillingly they complied.

And after a moment the dazed sarif picked up his dropped swords and faced the unmoving Wetlander's gauntness. Trapped at last he was and like a cornered sorap with broken wings he launched himself at Hardan.

Their swords met, clashed and sparks flew from their slithering blades. They broke and circled again, each wary for an opening that the other could not parry. Again and again the four swords rasped, yet from neither man was any blood drawn, so evenly were they matched. Nitka Porn's reach was the longer, but his bulk slowed down his speed, and it was here that Hardan saw his advantage.

Slowly he must wear down the big man, and the dry air that the huge Wetlander was not yet accustomed to breathing would do the rest. He would weaken, grow clumsy, and then his blade would find an opening.

But this Nitka Porn must have sensed. He swung his swords in a veritable hurricane of chopping steel and bore Hardan back against the rearing maars of the foremost wagon. A maar's forefoot lashed out, numbing Hardan's left shoulder, and the apish sarif's face glowed with devilish satisfaction. The success of his strategy so pleased him that he dropped his guard momentarily.

It was the opening Hardan needed. Gritting his teeth against the pain and numbness of his bruised shoulder he lunged upward with his left sword and his other blade darted in lightning strokes at the sarif's middle. His left hand jarred limply from the sword grip, but Nitka Porn staggered backward dying, the sword piercing deep into his eye-socket.

"Well done!" a hearty voice cried, and he turned to face a leather-husked captain of the Tarnish Guard with his remaining five men.

Ylda gave a little cry and in a moment was in the soldier's arms. A hot wave of jealousy burned within Hardan and then was gone.

"It is my father!" she cried gladly....

The sun was high overhead when they rode toward the crater valley of the Aarthmen where they were to spend another hand of days before guiding the wagon train on its way to the Bitter Sea. And now their purpose was to establish a treaty between Aarthmen and Wetlanders. Nor did Hardan fear that his small friends would receive any but fair treatment—their ability to read minds guarded them against that common failing of expanding races, to take what they wanted by treachery.

"We will guide the train to the Bitter Sea," he told Ylda as he loosed her from her bonds. "Some day all the Wetlands will be ours, and the men of Aarth will rule the Drylands, and ships-that-fly will link us together.

"But until then the trek must go on. Along this trail we are marking out other wagons will follow until a great road stretches here. There will be lakes and underground hostels along the way, and our children will travel in vurth-insulated wagons without maars, wagons faster than the wind.

"It was so on Aarth, their legends declare, and so it will be with us."

Ylda pouted. "What do we care about Aarth and treks?" she demanded. She nestled closer and her eyes closed contentedly.

Milton Keynes UK
Ingram Content Group UK Ltd.
UKHW030744071024
449371UK00006B/572